THE SOUND
OF LONELINESS

For

The androgynous poet Sappho,
whose legend for me became real
the winter of 2012 AD

THE SOUND OF LONELINESS
Poem Fragments

Pamela Preston

Marianne Press

Published by
Marianne Press
11230 Rivel, France
©Pamela Preston 2013
ISBN: 9781490458366

Custom, hand sewn and bound hard cover books
can be ordered directly from the publisher at
http://mariannepress.blogspot.com

Other titles published by Marianne Press:

Trilogy: Into the Goddesslands,
a memoir, 1993-2001
Book I,   200 pp
Book II,   200 pp
Book III, 120 pp

La Chanson de Pamé La Calmette,
an epic poem, 100 pp, 2002

Peasants and Poets,
a mythic novel, 360 pp, 2007

Gospel of the Cells,
poem and prose, 100 pp, 2009

Pâmoison,
a satiric novella, 130pp, 2011

All editions are printed, hand sewn and bound exclusively by
Marianne Press.

Introduction

I chose to spend a winter writing on an isolated beach in
Maine. My only diversions were the visits to my mother in an
independent living facility and a meeting with my elderly aunt.
My residency was to be alone time in the family beach house
but I was frequently visited by the ghosts of childhood past.
I had no idea what might come through my self-imposed
solitude. This little book is a testament to sounds lapping the
shore of my loneliness.

Pamela Preston
Maine
March, 2013

You may forget but

Let me tell you
this: someone in
some future time
will think of us

Sappho
Fragment #60

9/27/2012

Aye, Sappho

Your verse could be
a holy twitter:
Where are you
in our century?

1

There

I moved from south to north
suburban blares
of traffic
weed busters
blowers
mowers

Here
I tune my ears
to pounding surf

Joy comes

in the simplest tasks:
discarding trash
catching
a dream

.

Fright flees in the face

of what is right
This face/your face
smiles
dissolving fear

Terror moved

Into that southern cottage
broke the white picket fence
spit on foreign mountains

I knew loneliness

Aye, Sappho

How can I
be
who I am
in 2012?

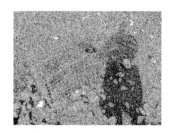

A few on my road

asked me to sing
I opened my pages
my mouth
my heart

Surprised
they cried
You are a real poet
I closed my book
Why?

9/28   Agèd Mother (i)

Your skin

like rice paper
falls in fragile folds
from your arm

I watch your bones
carry your skin
as you walk
carefully on dead feet
numbed by age

You live

In a place
of old ones
With them you hold
your memories at bay:
wild silent screams
forced down
Collective wisdom unheard

I ask

Where are you
but lost
in the dream of death

I ask

Who are you
when the words
you speak to me
request that I behave
as someone I am not

Still
I wait for kindness
that may
or may not come

9/29   Agèd mother (2)

Kindness did not come

Instead projectiles
garnished with guilt
heavy hit to the heart
My heart

I sorrowed

That after all these years
no change
Deranged, forgotten child
buried in the undergrowth
of withered weeds

9/30   Agèd mother (3)

It came

like a washing
first light:
I am sorry

10/1   Friend (1)

I sweat sickness

A fever in my mind
you hurt me
You stole my power
but it was I
who left my
Self
wide open
to your theft

When will I learn

not everyone
is fearless and forthcoming

The tide pulls

far back
leaving wastes
of wet sand
strewn with seaweed

Close in:
reflections
of a solitary gull

17

I stare forever

into tidal pools
finding temporary mirrors
and a sand crab
that died
a natural death

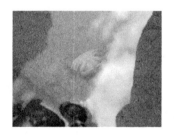

Sky over sea

Holds winds behind
clouds
sailing through
blue yellow light

10/5   Friend (2)

We hurt each other

Fear can strain to lies
This is not what
we really want

I learn

I can love you
That will be enough

At last

I have a room of my own
On my bed:
the poets
They remind me
who I am

Some day

when the tide pulls in
tightening the shore
swallowing rocks and kelp
your name
will be written
on what is left

10/6

Aye, Sappho

Can you fathom
this technology
this destruction?
Can I fathom
your soul
sweeping down
upon us
from antiquity?

The tides:
stronger than this
The moon knows all

10/08

Sappho, you said:

Strange to say

those who I treated
well are those who do
me the most wrong now

Christine, you said:

Je vis avec mes rêves
et mes envies

This house became

a projection festival
Possessed
by the needs of others
I learned
how to make a moat

10/8

Even though

some may wipe their feet
on your soul
some may not know you exist
some may obliterate you

I know you
That is enough

You may not know

where to go
Restore yourself
then you will know

10/19   Aging Aunt (1)

She heard a chorus

of 10,000 men
in the alley
on the rooftops
singing gospel

Singing hallelujah

Deaf

she put cotton in her ears
blocking out the truth
she knew:
the singing was
within her

A translucent angel

Fluttered nearby
The two of them
looked like twins

Her gaunt body

Did not worry me
nor her shouting demands
The louder her voice
the harder I listened

Great artist that she was

dissolved before my eyes
her skin wrapped bones
loosely
Where had her flesh gone?

Through her skeleton
whistled a wind
I had never heard
Her shouts were
all that was left

I knew

When her black eyes
glared at me
all the anger
of that helpless place

that she loved me the most

I cannot talk to her

right now
through her broken curtain
I can talk to her
through this:
her beauty
like a new veil
shimmers

10/20

I returned under blue skies

and a high tide
The fog rolled in
That night: thunder
Rain showered the sands
till dawn

10/21   Agèd Mother (4)

This time she stepped

gently down the hall
The colors of her blouse
black and red
A white scarf swayed
in her gait
Her smile: content

I was with her
Really with her

Bully boys

break boundaries
leave me raging
I say: watch out

Still
the sea
is strong enough

10/25　Agèd Aunt (2)

I am here to tell you

anger passed
like lightening from our lips
Her thunder words
dementia
clapped shut my mouth
Demons in their last stand
Surrender

Her illness

a furious wind
whipped in a new front
Stillness
promised warmth
from her everlasting soul

Something gasps

for breath
within her wracked body
I know who she is
I do not worry

This end is madness

Its vortex can only drive you
to a new beginning
I do not worry

Confusion of mind
is only mind
I do not worry

I knew you

when you were whole
I loved you

I know you
as you disintegrate
I love you more

The moment has come

to go forth
I light a candle for the poet
at night's lowest tide
The moon is half mast
stars drench the sea
and you anguish
in the belly of the whale

10/29

They call this the biggest storm

Sappho, sing to us
of catastrophic storms
before satellites

10/30

I caught a dream:

Garden bed
Mustard seed
Take root!

11/5

For the first time

I was cold
Primal fear
Winter survival

Gray skies swallow the sea

Gray floats on bare branches
Gray drains to damp chill
Gray suffocates

Winter looms

Bones shiver

The cold
has entered me

Light sinks

into the sea
at four pm
November

12/9   Shadow Sister

Archetypal icefall into

this body
this soul
this morning
My shadow
my sister

The child's anger

is mine
storming backward
in time
The obeisance of rhyme
meant nothing

I wanted to flee
to something
To summer

Dispel

Orual's ruse
with space
with grace

The sea today:

cobalt
lapping the pebbled shore
Inside
gales devalue me
I wrestle
sleepless in winter's shadows

Great light

casts a greater shadow
unknowingly
upon me
refusing solitude

Sappho, you muse over

blooming clover
star-strewn waters
Tortoise-shell harp in hand
hair violet plaited
you strum under
an ancient sun

Who is my sister, then?
The one who bargains
for my life
or
the one who sings
You are not forgotten

12/10

I find the rock cellar
aglow
Triassic stones
aglow

This stone
has your face
impressed upon it
That stone
sounds
of loneliness

12/14   Mother

Drawn to beauty

you teach me
that a long life
can bud
into flowers of innocence

I allow you
to show me
fear has no room
in acceptance

I rest on your couch

and listen to your stories
of worlds long past
while the naked trees
of winter
bloom

before the elder

You teach me

there is only one moment
and life is young
I only claim
these days with you
as our own
For now
we breathe easily

All Mothers
bless us now

12/20

I must not condemn

my weakness
Would God?

12/23

Once I opened the door

She saw not her daughter
but her mother
And I knew something called
her from beyond the curtain

12/25

This day a thaw

of snow and ice
Onto the shore
waves ebbed and flowed
A bottle rolled
from surf to sand
into my hand
Within it papyrus

A fragment

2013 Goodbyes

Fear crescendos

Take the ride
on the gust
drifting white
to the shed

Shed

The wind

wild with change
shakes attachments
From the tree
naked
trembling:
goodbye
before hello

I leave you:

ghosts of childhood
lurking in a winter house
You will play your tricks
long after I am gone

Fear ceases

facing the goodbye
to all I have loved here
to the sound I have heard here

Mother
you are in me now

There has been

erosion to what was
Make way
for what will be

The sea

has known all along:
this winter
these storms
your face/our face

A warmer sun

will dry salt tears
from this face
facing

departure

3/2013

I, Sappho

hear the loneliness
re sound
to here
You can only be
in the cacophony
of your century:
un sound

If you see the three

lilacs in their hair
barefoot running
through the field of dreams

If you hear

all the centuries
sound

If you smell

the salt
of the earth

If you taste

the salt
of the sea

If you touch

the hem
of the shore

If you behold

the fragment
in the bottle

Love

what is
waiting for you

Omega

Alpha